OUR VISIBLE GOD

PATRICIA ALDRIDGE-HINKLE

Inspiring Voices books may be ordered through booksellers or by contacting:

Inspiring Voices
1663 Liberty Drive
Bloomington, IN 47403
www.inspiringvoices.com
1 (866) 697-5313

ISBN: 978-1-4624-1208-2 (sc)
ISBN: 978-1-4624-1209-9 (e)

Print information available on the last page.

Inspiring Voices rev. date: 01/07/2019

InspiringVoices®

DEDICATION

This book is dedicated to the Glory of God, as He reveals Himself daily to those who have eyes of faith to see Him.

CONTENTS

OUR VISIBLE GOD IS SEEN

I   IN GRIEF

In All Things Give Thanks! 1

Consolation 3

You Are Not Alone 5

The Hole In The Sky 6

II   IN CHURCH

The Attic Window 8

Packing Up 9

III   IN UNEXPECTED PLACES

Invisible In Plain Sight 11

Pure Joy! 13

IV   IN NATURE

Music In The Sky 15

The Stink Lily 16

The Stink Bug 18

Suspended In Thin Air 20

A Walk In Autumn 22

V   IN FAMILY

Back In The Groove 24

Surprise! 25

Vigil 27

That's My Abby! 28

A Prayer For J.T. 30

Blessings Continue 33

VI   IN FEAR

Hawk On The Steeple 35

Death Threat 37

Pre-Flight Panic 38

Sub-Zero Angel 40

VII   IN A CHAOTIC WORLD

Food For Thought 42

Give Thanks 44

Thanksgiving Day Contrasts 46

Change 48

FOREWORD

Our life narrative is composed of a beautiful and complex tapestry consisting of our stories and heart songs. These are woven together to define who we are and how we have lived.

More than two decades ago, I was appointed to serve Wesley Memorial United Methodist Church. One of the first people I met was the Director of Music and Arts, Pat Aldridge. I instantly found in her a partner in ministry who shared a deep love for Christ and people. We worked together for nine years in serving the community around us and glorifying our Creator.

I was instantly amazed by Pat's diverse talents and gifts. She was an extremely talented musician who could draw from her choir music which exceeded their combined talents. Because they so loved her, they gave their all to the task of singing. The music that proceeded from the choir was a heavenly chorus each week.

Accompanying the choir were talented instrumentalists – organ, trumpets, French horn, cello and tympani - who were amazing. Even though the church was of a modest size, Pat put together an ensemble rivaling any church in the region. Even to this day, I long to have such a talented group playing in the church I serve. Each week the congregation was treated to a heavenly symphony that honored God.

Pat had a knack for writing and producing drama. Our church was known throughout upper East Tennessee for our Christmas productions. Several hundred people would grace our campus for dinner theater. They would leave with both their bellies and hearts filled to the brim. It was amazing because all who performed were amateurs, most of whom before working with Pat knew they had little or no acting abilities. She even placed me on stage. How did she get out of us what she did?

From every anthem and play Pat conducted, something special was communicated to the audience. We knew it was more than a technically performed work of art. It was Pat sharing her heart and passion with God and with us. We were so blessed to have a taste of heaven on earth.

While Pat's artistic flare was a blessing to me, another deep passion of her touched me more. Pat loved people and had an empathy which flowed into nearly all those she knew. Even though I carried the title of "pastor," in the congregation, it was Pat who had the "pastor's heart."

Early on in my ministry at the church, I felt as though Pat spent too much time and energy in caring for others. It seemed she always knew who was hurting and struggling and would share the information with me. I thought her level of concern and care she was providing would interfere with her primary job as our music and arts director.

I was so wrong. Never did the quality and timeliness of her work falter. Her prep for worship, preparing the choir, helping with the children and youth music ministries and Christian theater were always excellent.

Eventually, I came to realize God had given her the gift of compassion. She had so much love to share with others. Even to this day, Pat's love for others has not dimmed but continues to shine brightly. When we talk, she will share what is going on in the lives of others.

Pat's first husband was a key leader in the congregation and was loved by all. He was a spiritual giant in the church and in the community. He was a great ally. Pat and Duard were the perfect couple. They so deeply loved and supported each other.

The tapestry of our lives is often given its most brilliant colors when pain is woven into its pattern. Our agony becomes a contrast shading the work of art.

I had made plans to attend a conference with my father and another colleague. Pat had assured me all would be well at the church during my absence. She was sure the staff could manage quite well without me. (She was right because they did a great job).

So, with all my preparations made, we set off one morning for Atlanta. Little did I know that within an hour of my departure, Pat received a call informing her of her husband's collapse. It would be just a matter of a few minutes that she would learn he could not be revived.

I would not learn of Duard's death for several hours after my arrival in Atlanta. (This was before my cell phone was a constant companion.) When I heard the news, my heart sank. I contacted Pat as quickly as possible. I knew I could not return immediately because of traveling with others. As I talked with Pat, I could feel she was heartbroken, yet she was so understanding of my situation and showed more compassion toward me than I had been able to express for her.

Grief was so real to my sister. She never tried to run from it but seemed to run into it knowing she would emerge stronger at some point. While some of her heart songs had notes of melancholy, her heart never stopped singing.

Some years after I left Wesley Memorial I was talking with a mutual friend. He shared with me Pat was marrying a widower from the area. I did not know the man and I felt it was important for me to approve. But Pat did not consult with me, nor did I have opportunity to interview her new groom.

When I met Clark, I first thought, "Man, you are blessed!" Then as I got to know him, I realized he is a blessing to Pat. She was given another opportunity to share her life with a great man.

Many of the stories and poems you will read in this book are a part of my life experience with Pat. As I read them, my memories come alive and my heart sings. I imagine being present in those events I did not have the fortune to enjoy with Pat. My narrative of my life and the strength of my heart have been uplifted by sharing life with Pat.

I know you will be fed and enriched as you read these stories and heart songs. You will find yourself soaring and at times weeping. You will remember your stories and hum your own heart songs. Maybe, if you are lucky, you will be able to find a vantage point from which you can view your own life tapestry.

Dr. Dwight Kilbourne
Senior Pastor
Ooltewah United Methodist Church
Ooltewah, Tennessee

PREFACE

Have you seen God? No? Yes? Perhaps? How can we "see" God? Is not God, Whom we worship, unlimited in size, shape, and scope? Does not His all-encompassing love and the fact that He is omnipotent, omnipresent, and omniscient give Him the ability to be seen at all times, by all people, and in all places? Yes, if we are looking through the eyes of faith that only He can give us. As creatures formed in God's own image, I do believe that God can and does reveal (makes visible) Himself to us through all our senses.

When I was about five years old, my mother took me to the woods to get rich dirt for the many flowers she grew around our home. I was amazed to find beautiful flowers blooming everywhere in the woods. As I ran from plant to plant inspecting each colorful blossom, I was confused, because I knew that Mother worked very hard to grow her flowers. I asked my mother who planted the flowers. She replied, "God did!"

That was the first time that I "saw" the hand of God in nature. It made a lasting impression on me! It is my prayer that my life narrative will help you to see *OUR VISIBLE GOD* often in your daily routine. Each encounter brings me peace and joy!

ACKNOWLEDGMENT

Without the enthusiasm and encouragement of my family and many friends, *OUR VISIBLE GOD* would not have been written. Thank you for believing in the concept and content. Also, thanks to the Inspiring Voice Consultants for their insight and patience in the publishing process. The encouragement of my former pastor, Dr. Dwight Kilbourne, and my family provided the focus and confidence to complete this project. The love and effort of my daughter, Melanie, and my husband, Clark, as well as his brilliant family (whose technical knowledge rescued me countless times when I was at war with my computer) kept me going. Thanks also go to Sarrah, at Bays Media, for her expertise in submitting the photos. When I was floundering in my efforts to pull all the loose ends together after the book was finished, my "Alabama Angel" friend, Pam, came for a visit, rescuing me with her humor, patience, and literary experience, and helping with the final copy submission. You are reading the result of constant prayers of many people. I ask that the prayers continue for all who read *OUR VISIBLE GOD!*

INTRODUCTION

This book is very personal. Dr. Dwight Kilbourne, a former pastor of mine, calls it a "Life Narrative." My family tree is filled with ancestors who served the Lord gladly. My grandfather was a minister, and his father was a circuit rider in Tennessee, so it is no surprise that I was introduced to God as soon as I could comprehend.

I have had many experiences in my life when I have felt guided or led in a particular direction to an unexpected situation or person. Other times I have found myself in unexplained circumstances or called to minister to a stranger. For many years, I felt that my relationship with God was not to be shared. Some of my experiences I even tried to protect from exploitation or misinterpretation.

Some time ago, I was led to begin sharing my journey with others in similar circumstances. These narratives cover the full spectrum of my emotions, including wonder, fear, grief, illness, and unbelievable joy with the people God has placed in my life. Each experience and friend has made God even more "VISIBLE" to me! I pray that this book will help you to "see" God daily, as I do!

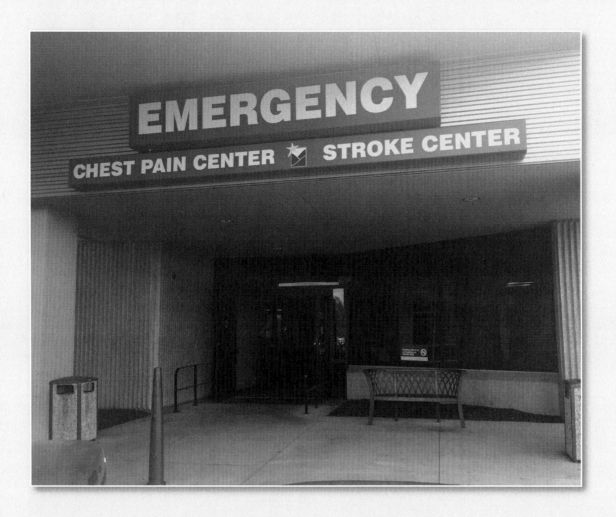

IN ALL THINGS GIVE THANKS!

My husband, Duard, and I enjoyed our breakfast alone that morning. We usually enjoyed our meals with our son, Jeff, his wife, Tembra, and our three grandchildren, Nyela, Megan and Natalie. They were living with us temporarily while their new house was being built. Today, however, we had our breakfast alone a little early because Duard was substitute teaching, as he often did since retiring from teaching ten years earlier after surviving a massive heart attack. I credited his recovery to the grace of God, the prayers of church and community, and a fantastic doctor and rehab team! As he finished getting ready, I remained in the kitchen to clean up after our breakfast.

When he was ready to leave, he came into the kitchen for our "Goodbye Ritual," which included a sweet kiss, a big hug, and a "Have a great day, Honey!" He left the kitchen, and I returned to my cleaning. Moments later he returned for another "Goodbye Ritual." We hugged and kissed again, and he was on his way to school, as I headed out the door for my job at our church.

Shortly after lunch I received a call from Jeff. Duard was in the ER at the hospital and they were trying to find my office number. I immediately knew that he was dead. Had he been alive, he would have told them my number! A co-worker drove me to the hospital. As I entered the ER, a wonderful Christian male nurse friend, with whom I had served on several mission weekends, was standing with arms outstretched just inside the door. I collapsed in his arms.

He led me to the trauma room where Duard's body lay. He seemed to just be sleeping. His body was still warm. Family and friends crowded in, and we wept together. One by one they left the cubicle, and I was alone with my dear husband. He had suffered a fatal heart attack! Yet a very powerful thought immediately popped into my brain: "IN ALL THINGS GIVE THANKS!"

I was stunned! My brain shot back, "Lord, surely you don't expect me to give thanks when the love of my life is lifeless on this gurney!"

Suddenly another very powerful, yet tender, gentle and loving response gained control of my thoughts: *"But I gave you ten extra years!"*

I walked to Duard's side, picked up his hand and began to stroke his arm as I told him just how thankful I was to God for bringing us together about 40 years earlier. I told him what a magnificent man God had given me in response to my childhood prayers for a loving husband when I grew up. I gave thanks for our fun days of courtship as college students, our marriage, Army days, and the indescribable joy of God's giving us our two children, Jeff and Melanie, now amazing adults! When I reminded Duard of family trips and pranks we had played on each other, I almost laughed out loud! If any nurses were watching me, they must have thought I had lost my mind! I realized that God had packed our last ten years together with love, laughter, good times, and blessings too numerous to count! Looking back to that day I realized that our time alone in that trauma room was a healing gift from God.

God, You had answered my frantic prayer ten years earlier when I prayed that You would keep Duard alive because his family, especially his grandchildren needed him. You also answered Duard's prayer, which was that he would be able to live his life so that all would know that he had lived it to the fullest.

Thank You, God! You have shown Yourself to be visible in life and in death. Therefore, I will

"IN ALL THINGS GIVE THANKS!"

"In everything give thanks, for this is the will of God in Christ Jesus."

1Thessalonians 5:18 NKJV

CONSOLATION

Where do I turn? What can I do
To ease this pain that seems to pierce me through and through?
All hope is gone; all dreams have fled.
There is so much more that I wish I could have said.
How this can be, I'll never know.
I only know that I now have no place to go.

Gone are the good times we thought would never end.
Even in bad times we could share friend to friend.
But now my heart aches with such great pain
Because I know these times will never come again.

I turn to You, Lord. I know You're here.
Your perfect love is sent to overcome my fear.
Your strength is mine each time I call.
I know that You'll restore me every time I fall.
My future now rests in Your hands.
I know that You have good for me in all Your plans.

~~~~~~~~~~

I will praise Your name with every breath,
For now I know You've conquered death.

I have friends on earth and friends above,
And we all are alive in the light of Your love!

So, heal me, Lord. Draw me closer to You,
And I will serve as You ask me to do.
This peace You give I now can see.
It does not depend on what happens to me.
I thank You, Dear God, for memories sweet,
And I look to the day when we again shall meet.

(I wrote this song for solo voice and dancer, with organ and flute accompaniment,
in memory of my late husband, Duard Paul Aldridge.)

YOU ARE NOT ALONE

When Saturday dawned, I awoke to find myself in the middle of a huge pity party. I was in Colorado to attend my nephew's wedding. That weekend would have been the 40th wedding anniversary of my late husband and me. I had tried to be brave the last year and a half since his death, but that day I woke up weeping – a basket case! I could not shake a feeling of being totally alone, a feeling I had never experienced.

When we arrived at the church, the business of others scurrying around with last minute wedding preparations only flooded my memory with our own wedding day, our happiness, our love, and my deep grief of losing him. For the first time in my life, I experienced acute loneliness. I wandered through the beautiful church while taking candid shots of the wedding party and snapping pictures of the massive sanctuary with its magnificent organ and pipes.

I finally settled into a center pew to watch a florist create a lovely arrangement on the impressive elevated altar. The result was truly beautiful, so I took a picture of it. I then moved to the right aisle and snapped a shot from that angle. My morose mood lasted throughout the entire ceremony (through which I wept), the reception, and the remainder of the evening. The rest of our Colorado trip was very pleasant.

Later, back home, as I thumbed through my newly developed seven rolls of film taken on the trip, the sight of the two altar pictures literally took my breath away. The Cloud above the altar had NOT been in my view finder, yet it had shifted with me as I moved to the aisle! Suddenly, a feeling of peace and contentment settled over me as my mind was filled with scripture: our being surrounded by such a great Cloud of Witnesses, the Cloud which led the Israelites out of Egypt, the Cloud of Presence which filled The Tabernacle, the Cloud which covered Mount Sinai when the Ten Commandments were given to Moses, the Cloud covering the Mount of Transfiguration, and the Cloud in which Jesus ascended into Heaven. These thoughts left me with the feeling of humility and thanksgiving.

WOW GOD! You were there with me that entire day, and I was too full of self- pity to realize it! Forgive me Lord. I will never feel alone again. Thank You, Jesus!

". . . and lo, I am with you always, even to the end of the world."
Matthew 28:20 KJV

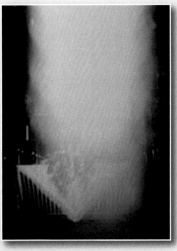

THE HOLE IN THE SKY

My husband, Clark, and I were headed home after a disheartening visit with his deceased wife's mother, Pauline. I had fallen in love with Pauline, her three remaining daughters, and her son when I first met them several years ago.

Pauline was in her late 80's when I met her. She was a beautiful lady, a talented artist, and a writer who used her computer to send her family a monthly newsletter filled with jokes, stories, and memories. She was also a gardener who lived alone in her own home on her own farm with her many flowers, apple and walnut trees, and her vegetable garden, which was down the hill and across a creek. She canned her produce in a heavy pressure cooker in her small kitchen.

At age 94, she was in her yard admiring spring flowers when she fell and broke her hip. Her active life suddenly changed from her being independent and driving her car, to a life filled with hospitals, surgery, nursing home, and finally back home on hospice at age 96. Until recently, she was still trying to remain active with simple strengthening exercises, helping to solve crosswords puzzles, singing hymns with me, and talking with family and friends around her kitchen table.

Today, however, had been different. She was extremely weak and could not communicate or even squeeze our hands. She could no longer get out of bed. It was obvious to all that she was very low. Her hospice nurses agreed that she could go at any time. We said our goodbyes and began our drive back to our home in an adjoining county. It was hard to leave her, even for an important meeting that evening. Our hearts were heavy.

As we came to a long, straight stretch of highway not far from Pauline's house, an unusual cloud formation loomed before us. In front of a cloud bank was a bright yellow cloud. Its shape resembled a shrouded figure with outstretched arms. Above the yellow figure was a large, blue hole in the darker cloud. I immediately felt that Pauline had just died, and I called back to her home to see if she were still alive. We were relieved to learn that she had rallied a bit and was again responsive.

Looking back at the cloud, I pondered what message it had for us. I felt at peace as I realized that my sweet Pauline would be in a "Holding Pattern" until God was ready to "pull her through that hole into heaven." There may be countless facets in our lives and unfinished relationships which need to be resolved--which are unknown to us and known only to God. Our earthly lives are based on incomplete knowledge and understanding. For me, that is where trust in God takes over. Who are we to worry or fret over God's timing in our lives or our deaths? Why spend time grieving over a death that has not happened? Instead, why not rejoice and give thanks for each day God gives us to spend with our loved ones on this earth?

Thank You, Lord, for the countless loved ones in my life, through whom I have clearly seen Your love.

"To everything there is a season, and a time for every purpose under
heaven: A time to be born, and a time to die;"

Ecclesiastes 3:1-2 NKJV

(Pauline passed through her own "Hole in the Sky" on Sunday, May 15, 2016, a month before her 97th birthday. She left a wealth of humorous newsletters, a book, countless beautiful paintings, much wisdom, and sweet memories in the hearts of family and friends.)

THE ATTIC WINDOW

Our church is rather modern, with clean lines and a vaulted ceiling over the congregation. Because of my position as Director of Music for 40 plus years, I have spent much more time in the choir loft, which has a huge stained glass attic window above it, unseen from the congregation, but visible to the choir. After dark the light through the attic window on our hill focuses a heavenly spotlight on the surrounding community.

I am not in the choir loft today. Here I sit on the back pew of the congregation. I am recovering from a serious, painful illness, and I lack the strength to sing. But my heart is singing! I am giving thanks, because God has brought me through this illness, and I am on the road to recovery! God has brought me to His beautiful sanctuary this morning to worship Him in all His power and glory!

As I bask in His comforting sunlight today as it bathes the cross, I am taken back to my many years as Director of Music when I stood before the cross to direct inspiring anthems Sunday after Sunday. More times than I could count, as I led the choir on cloudy days to the glorious climax of a powerful anthem, God would suddenly send His heavenly shaft of sunlight through the clouds and stained glass attic window, projecting stunning images and shadows on the cross and choir precisely on the exact beat the music reached its soul-stirring climax! This often resulted in tears of joy—just like today from the back pew!

What a loving God we serve! Thank You, Lord!
Help me to be like that attic window, through which Your light shines to bless and inspire others!

"In the same way, let your light shine before others,
So that they may see your good works and give glory to your Father in heaven."
Matthew 5:16 NIV

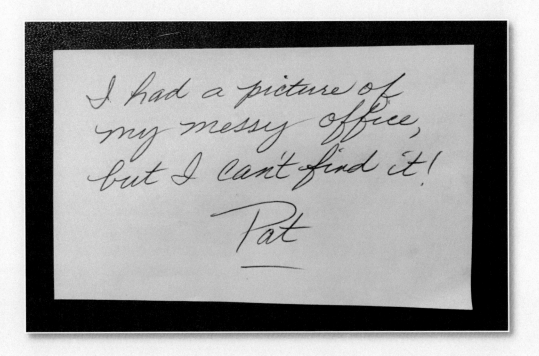

I had a picture of
my messy office,
but I can't find it!
Pat

PACKING UP

(After 40 plus years as Music Director at
Wesley Memorial United Methodist Church,
Johnson City, Tennessee)

Well, I've put it off as long as I can, I guess.
Lord, what am I going to do with all this mess?
Forty plus years of my life surround me,
And the countless boxes of "STUFF" astound me!

"Why on earth do I keep things?" I mutter
As I stumble and stagger amid all the clutter.
"Why can't I learn to throw stuff away—
Just toss it all out and start a new day?"

Here are books, magazines, and music galore,
Instruments, notebooks and phonebooks–(four)!
LP's, cassettes and a zillion CD's,
Plus pictures, videos and yes, DVD'S.

Eleven plants and a large gumdrop tree,
Vases, boxes, and baskets must go home with me.
Where I will put them I haven't a clue!
"Lord!" I cry out, "What shall I do?"

"You must learn to discern," I felt the Lord say.
"Some things you should keep and not throw away.
Those things which remind you of people so dear
Will inspire and comfort and should always be near.
The things you should toss will not draw you to Me,
Nor help you to witness to all those you see.

Keep only the tools you will need to sow seeds
Of love and compassion to meet the world's needs.
Hold on to the friendships, good memories and fun,
The laughter, the music, the good that's been done.
When I placed you at Wesley, I knew you would grow
In spiritual ways you then could not know."

My heart became lighter, my task not so large.
I knew that the Lord, and not I, was in charge.
So, thank You, Lord, for Your love through the years,
And standing by me in the fun times and tears.

*Written with much love to my Wesley family and to God, who made Himself
visible to me in countless ways and through countless people.*

"Praise ye the Lord. Praise God in His sanctuary: Praise Him in the firmament of His power.
Praise Him for his mighty acts: Praise Him according to His excellent greatness."

Psalm 150:1-2 KJV

INVISIBLE IN PLAIN SIGHT

The beauty of autumn often overwhelms me! However, some people I know begin to dive into depression when the first leaf falls. I really pity those folks, because they are missing one of God's greatest gifts, as He gleefully spatters paint from His paint brush with abandonment. Long walks on crisp days are exciting for me, but I equally enjoy the countless colors I can see on three sides of my sunroom. Breath-taking beauty!

One day I was working in the sunroom when my husband, Clark, made a comment about how well our calico cat, Callie, blended in with her surroundings. I rose from my chair and walked to his side at the door leading to the patio. Past the patio were woods filled with vivid colors of oak, maple, sumac, and nut trees, which grow on a high ridge beside our home. I looked out the door, but I could not find Callie.

"She is right over there!" my husband said, but I saw nothing but leaves-- beautiful leaves! Finally, he showed me where she was--as plain as day, once he revealed her location by giving me some hints for zeroing in on her.

I do believe that, more often than not, God is on our every side, surrounding and protecting us with the profound love only He can give, yet we cannot see or feel His presence, even when we are actively seeking Him! Perhaps we are not expecting Him to be that close in our lives. Sometimes He is seen in "unholy places", ministering to people with whom we do not want to even associate. Could it be that we sometimes do not want to see Jesus, or is it that we do not want Jesus to see us in compromising circumstances?

Are there measurable factors or daily routines that could help us grow closer and open our senses to His presence? Often the cacophony of our multiple televisions, radios, cellular devices, plus our countless activities and financial concerns drown out that "still, small voice" of God that spoke our world into being when He created us to be His companions for eternity.

Could we "see" God more clearly if we sat alone in silence, praying that He would reveal His presence in our lives? Maybe it would help us to see with our spiritual eyes the Mighty God who surrounds and resides within us at all times. Perhaps then HIS will would become clearer, and we would be able to follow HIS plan joyfully, instead of worrying about our future.

Lord, please give me spiritual eyes to see and appreciate Your presence in my life each day.

"For I know the plans I have for you," declares the Lord, Plans to prosper
you and not to harm you, Plans to give you hope and a future."

Jeremiah 29:11 NIV

Did you find Callie? She is there. Look for a spot of white.

PURE JOY!

"Consider it pure joy," I read, "whenever you face trials."
"Perseverance is the promised reward at the end of tortuous miles."
I'm not too sure that I want to go there. Joy's supposed to be FUN!
Why can't I just laugh and have a good time, then sleep when day is done?

The weekend was near when I read those words, and I was expecting guests—
Wonderful friends from out of state—my house must look its best.
What fun we would have with all that we'd planned. Oh, I could hardly wait
To taste the delicious dinner I'd cook, but then they called. They'd be late.

"No problem," I said, "We will just go out as soon as you get here".
It turned out great, for we just ate at a restaurant that was near.
Fine food and fellowship filled the body, not to mention the soul,
As we laughed and talked and reminisced, forgetting that we were old.

A good night's rest, a glorious morning, and I was the first one up.
But when I turned on the faucet, I got NO WATER—not even a cup!
No showers, no coffee, no breakfast, no joke! There was nothing else to do.
So we went out to breakfast and stuffed ourselves, and we enjoyed that, too.

Not knowing that another "joy" awaited, that night we prepared for bed,
Till one guest yelled, and we came running. "The bathroom's flooded!" she said.
And was it ever! The sewage was rising on the floor, also in the tub.
No plumber makes house calls at midnight, and that, my friend, was the rub.

So we did what anyone else would have done: We laughed and joked and mopped.
And thanked the Lord that somehow all the water finally stopped.
The next three days ran on "Plan B", but we laughed and had great fun.
And, when they left, we all could see PERSEVERANCE HAD WON!

*Oh, Lord, thank You for showing Yourself to us through Your gift of laughter, which
enables us to refrain from taking ourselves and situations too seriously.*

"A merry heart doeth good like a medicine, but a broken spirit drieth the bones."

Proverbs 17:22 KJV

MUSIC IN THE SKY

It was late afternoon on a crisp fall day as Clark, my husband, and I drove west on Interstate 81 to visit family. Traffic was fairly heavy as I glanced up at the partly cloudy sky. Suddenly, I was fumbling for my phone to snap an unbelievable picture! That phone! It always sank to the bottom of my purse just when I needed it quickly! I finally found it and focused it toward the sky, which, of course, was blocked as we were passing a semi!

As we know, clouds can change shapes quickly, according to the wind flow. What I originally saw was a series of many notes in a line across the sky. Heavenly music! I was very excited as I tried to focus around the semi to our right! By the time I was able to get a clear shot, several of the notes had faded, and more were on their way, but I was able to get a shot of a quarter and eighth note rhythm. As a former music teacher, I was elated!

This happened as advent was approaching, so I immediately thought of the angel chorus in the heavens when the birth of Jesus was announced to the shepherds. When I shared the photos with a friend, he sang, "first day of Christmas!" As a musician, he immediately recognized the rhythm pattern without my prompting.

The following week in an Advent Bible Study, our homework was to share with the group two images which were etched on our heart and how they related to Advent and Christmas. One of my shared images was, of course, my picture of "Music in the Sky," which reminded me of the angels' appearance to the shepherds that "First Day of Christmas!"

Lord, thank You for Your gift of music, an international language, which unites all people to praise You!

"The heavens declare the glory of God; The skies proclaim the work of his hands."

Psalm 19:1 NIV

THE STINK LILY

One day, as my sister-in-law, Brenda, and I worked in her mother's yard in late spring, I spotted a remarkable plant growing close to the side door. I had never seen anything like it! I immediately went to investigate. Its single blossom was huge, with a rippled edge. Its surface was velvety and vivid in hues of pink, red, purple, and blue.

Brenda did not know its name, but she said that it had been there for years. I later asked Brenda's mother about the beautiful plant. It seems that a friend had given the plant to her husband many years ago. The friend called it a "Stink Plant," which explained the strange odor I had smelled when I approached it.

Later I researched the mysterious plant, whose odor resembled rotting flesh. I learned that its genus was "Dracunculus" and its species was "Vulgaris." Other common names were listed, two of which were: "Dragon Lily" and "Stink Lily." I did not understand how such a stunning plant could be commonly known as a "Stink Lily."

This started a strange thought process in my brain. Did God make this beautiful plant to be stinky, or did He make the stinky plant to be beautiful? Obviously, He intended it to be both. Then I thought of the skunk, a very photogenic little creature who is extremely "stinky" in order to repel its many enemies. Next I thought of other creatures (some people) whose "stinky" nature attracts, rather than repels. It all seemed to be in the eye of the beholder.

Next thought: Did God include something special in our DNA when He created us in His image that is especially "stinky" to our enemy, the devil, yet endearing to God? I believe that He did! I believe that our love and obedience to our Father is so repulsive to the devil that he flees from our presence when he perceives it. Satan sees beauty only in our sin and disrespect to God. God is saddened by it. God sees our love for Him as beautiful. To the devil our devotion to God acts as a repellant, sending him away like a roaring lion, seeking weaker souls whom he can capture in their sin!

Dear God, help us to be truly beautiful in Your eyes, but real "stinkers" in the devil's eyes!

"… Your accuser, the devil, is on the prowl like a roaring lion, seeking someone to devour."

1 Peter 5:8 CEB

THE STINK BUG

My weekly schedule is usually packed with family, church, and community activities. However, for the past several weeks all activities had come to a screeching halt. My body had been attacked by a serious bacteria that could turn septic, if not treated as soon as possible with powerful antibiotics! My urologist reacted quickly with two powerful antibiotics, taken together morning and night. Before beginning the medications I thought I carefully read all the fine print in the instructions and side effects lists. Throughout the week, I took note as the side effects began to appear: diarrhea (check), tingling, numbness, and pain in an arm (check), and a painful, itchy rash on the affected arm (check).

When the side effects became unbearable, I returned to the antibiotic fine print to reread it. What I did NOT read the first time stated that the antibiotic should be stopped IMMEDIATELY if the pain and numbness occurred. OOPS! I had completed the full week's dosage, even though the side effects began midweek. The result of my carelessness was intense pain for several weeks, which confined me to my home. I was forced to sleep sitting upright because it was too painful to lie down. Naturally, I was totally exhausted and frustrated! My daily Bible reading was taking me through the book of Job, with which I could really relate! Like Job, I was questioning why this torture was lasting so long.

One day in early autumn, I took my devotional books to our patio table. I realized, as I began to read, that the wind was a little too stiff for comfort. I decided to continue outside, anyway. My reading was suddenly interrupted when a large stink bug came zooming in on the breeze and landed directly in front of me......ON HIS BACK!!

He was in a panic as he wriggled and squirmed in his effort to get back on his feet! Just as I was about to flick him to an upright position, all movement ceased! I stared at his motionless body for a long time and assumed that he had died. To my surprise, he suddenly flipped himself over and was gone with the wind, after his time of rest.

A smile automatically lit up my face. "Lord," I asked silently. "Did You send me out to the patio so that I could see that stink bug land in front of me with a message from You? Am I like that stink bug, frantically thrashing in endless activity while accomplishing nothing? Were You telling me that I need to be still and know that You are God, so that I can regain my strength to serve You better? If so, I get the message! Thank You, Lord!"

Oh, Lord! Help me to recognize the opportunities for rest which You place in my busy days.

"Be still, and know that I am God."

Psalm 46:10 NIV

SUSPENDED IN THIN AIR

Sometimes God gives us optical illusions, which can really play with our minds. Such was the case one morning in my sunroom as I lingered over my breakfast.

It was a beautiful, sunny fall day with a gentle breeze when I glanced across the room to my right toward the patio door I looked back at my food, then did a double-take as I jerked my head toward the door again!

There, perfectly framed in the glass door, was a large oak leaf—dancing in thin air! Now, I had seen countless dancing leaves in my lifetime, but all the others eventually drifted to the ground. This particular oak leaf did not! I crossed the room and stood at the door. I could see nothing attached to the leaf. It continued to dance, as if on a stage, lifting itself high in the air, then dipping low. It turned and twirled—to the left—to the right, perfectly choreographed. I felt extremely blessed to be witnessing this!

I opened the door and stepped out to the patio to get a closer look. Still I could see nothing holding the leaf. Then, as I stepped back into the room, the sun rose over the roof of the sunroom, and I caught a quick glint off something in the air. I again went outside to investigate. I found a perfectly logical explanation, which sent my brain spinning at the wonder of one of the smallest of God's little critters. What I saw was as astounding as the dancing leaf itself.

From the top point of our folded patio umbrella in the center of the table a tiny spider had woven her thread, which extended about 12 feet over to the corner of the sunroom roof. Midway between the umbrella and the roof hung a single, almost invisible, perpendicular filament which had snagged the wandering oak leaf, enabling its leaps and pirouettes as the wind's choreography dictated.

The oak leaf danced throughout the day until dark. The next morning I rushed to see if the leaf had danced all night. It had not. It had made its exit sometime during the night, and a colorful maple leaf had taken the stage to continue the dance! Throughout the day the maple leaf danced tirelessly. I wondered just what kind of leaf was waiting in the wings to take the stage on day three. However, the show was cancelled after only two performances, which were so magnificent that I shall never forget them!

Thank You, God, for inviting me to not just one, but two stunning performances!

"Praise him with tambourine and dance…"

Psalm 150:4 NRSV

A WALK IN AUTUMN

"It's autumn, Lord, and it makes my heart glad
To view so much color! I will not be sad!
Splendor and grandeur are all I can see
Through showers and sunshine, wherever I be."

White clouds dot a sky of Columbia blue,
Encircled by bright leaves of every known hue.
The brisk air invites me to go for a walk
Down a leaf-covered path while my Lord and I talk.

"I love you, my child," I hear the Lord say.
"Relax and enjoy my gift of this day!"
"I thank You, Dear God, for all that You give:
Your love and forgiveness that we all might live!"

"But I'm getting older, though my heart still feels young,
And I have many songs that remain to be sung.
I think of my mother, who taught me Your Grace.
Yet her memory deserted her beautiful face!"

"Lord, sometimes I do have concerns for my mind,
With lost keys and purses – so much I can't find!
Will I, too, lose my memories so dear,
As my body grows feeble and death draws near?"

But then I remember Mom's last things to go:
Memorized Scriptures and the hymns she loved so!
She started each morning with "This Is the Day,"
Witnessing to caregivers the joy of your way!

Then I feel the Lord's Presence, and I'm covered with peace,
Surrendering concerns to His blessed release!
The worst of times He can turn into good,
And He'll guide me through, as He said He would!

"Autumn, My Child, is the womb of the spring.
Its falling leaves nourish the seeds with its rain.
A time of rest and for growth is essential
If a passing soul is to reach its potential!"

"Remember that death is the door to tomorrow.
The loved ones you've lost are in joy, not in sorrow!
Focus on Me each day of your life,
And I'll travel beside you through each day of strife!"

And so I walk on with a smile on my face,
Thankful that God and I share this space.
"I love you, My Child!" I hear the Lord say.
"Relax and enjoy My gift of this day!"

Thank You, Lord, for walking with me this morning!

"But seek ye first the kingdom of God and his righteousness…"

Matthew 6:33 KJV

As far back as I can remember my family ranked second only to God in importance and respect in my life. The prayers of my Godly parents guided me through serious physical challenges in my infancy and early childhood. Because of this, I was introduced to the love and power of God from birth, for which I am eternally grateful! My sister, Carolyn and I knew that we were blessed to grow up in a loving, stable home, and both of us were fortunate to marry men who shared our beliefs and values. Her husband's first name is Duard. (God has a sense of humor, because as a child I prayed for a husband just like Duard!)

When my husband, Duard, died suddenly, I discovered that I had many families, not just my family and Duard's family. I also had my church, my neighborhood, and community, plus high school and college classmates, who became like family to rally around us in prayer, love, and support to help us get back on our feet again. I felt God's presence and strength as never before in my life, as He revealed to me just how large my family really was, and how great was God's love! It was during this time that I also learned that each day was much more fun and productive when God, not I, was in control. That novel idea was a real life-changer!

I would like to say that I have always been faithful since then to return that love and support to other grieving families, but that would be a lie, because I have not. I loved and appreciated these people, and my intentions were good, but far too often, I allowed less important matters and tasks to control my priorities and time. Somehow, even with all my shortcomings and failure to return all the good deeds to others, God returned to me a sense of normalcy, and I was able to pick up my life and allow happiness to again permeate my being. God and "my many families" put me back in the groove to be in His service to others once more.

Lord, thank You for caring families of friends and neighbors.
Thanks for Your restorative powers, and help me to refrain from procrastination.
Please make Yourself visible in establishing priorities and in my time management
so that I may be of greater service to You and others in time of need.

"Strive first for the kingdom of God and His righteousness, and
all these things will be given to you as well."

Matthew 6:33 NRSV

SURPRISE!

Ten productive years passed since my husband's death. They were filled with family activities, which usually included food, sports, musical activities, concerts, and travel. My family, Jeff, his wife, Tembra and Melanie always tried to include me in their travel and vacations. Family cruises were great! God gave each member of my family a double portion of good humor, so the rafters often rang with laughter whenever we gathered at home or were on an outing. I still missed my husband, but with family and work, I was content.

My position as a church director of music was hectic, yet very rewarding. The choir was talented, large, and enthusiastic. We were also blessed with fine organist and keyboard talent, as well as orchestra and handbells. Those who served in the music ministry were dedicated to serve and witness however and whenever needed. These talented adventurers would tackle published, as well as original music, which included original and published cantatas, and dinner theater musicals. At Christmas, we invited members of the congregation to join us for the dinner theater production musical.

I was a very busy person with church, community, and family responsibilities, all of which I enjoyed! God's presence was felt, and His hand was seen in the music program of our church. I was humbled and thankful to be a part of it. I had no time nor desire to include anyone else in my life. I knew that no one could ever replace my late husband, so I never took the time to look, much less date. I was very content with church and family.

Then, with no warning, a gentleman unexpectedly appeared. He, too, had lost a loving spouse to a heart attack several years before. He also had two children, a boy and a girl, as I did. I had met him shortly after his wife died, but had never really talked with him, and he didn't even remember meeting me. Besides, I was not looking for anyone or anything else in my life.

A few years later, we happened to be seated across from each other at a barbeque. I immediately sensed his pain and knew that he was still struggling with the death of his wife, Barbara. He had dated some since her death and was heavily involved with church work, was 1st chair trombone in the community band, and hosted foreign exchange students. I learned that he loved music and sports, which were my main interests, as well. I also discovered that he was a praying man. Yet he was still grieving and hurting, though he tried not to show it. We were still talking after everyone else had left the table.

Sometime later we met again at the funeral of a mutual musician friend, and he asked me to sit with him. After the funeral, neither of us had eaten dinner, so we decided to grab a bite to eat at a nearby restaurant when we left the church. I am sure that we drew some attention. There we were… talking the night away… two "certified seniors" among the last to leave an establishment frequented by the college crowd at that hour.

Almost two years later, Clark Hinkle and I were married. We are very different in many ways. He is a night owl; I am out of bed at the crack of dawn. He can work at his computer with the television and a CD blaring; I must have absolute quiet in order to think and work at my computer. His brain is wired more like that of a chemist or engineer. I am more social and a "people" person, so sometimes communication is both comical and challenging! I try to choose my words wisely, but sometimes I tease him by telling him I think that God forgot to put a filter between his brain and his mouth. He is patient, kind, and good natured. He never knew what sarcasm was until he met me! Yes, we are very different, but we love each other and are so thankful that God brought us together!

Much has happened in the last nine years, and countless times we have thanked God that we have each other to lean on, confide in, travel and work, play and worship together. Do we still love our first spouses? Yes, definitely! Sometimes, he calls me "Barbara," and sometimes I call him "Duard," but that's OK! We each consider it a compliment, because our marriage reflects the respect, love, and total comfort in each other's presence, just as we had in our first marriages. GOD IS GOOD!

Thank You, Lord, for bringing this kind, patient man into my life. Please continue to increase our love for each other and You, Father, as You lead us daily into Your service.

"And now these three remain: faith, hope, and love. But the greatest of these is love."

1 Corinthians 13:13 NIV

The night was dark. The night was long.

Time moved slowly.

We chatted awhile, then dozed off and on.

Time moved slowly.

Nurses came. Nurses went.

Time moved slowly.

Dawn approached. Traffic increased.

Time moved slowly

"It won't be long now." The nurse announced.

Time moved slowly.

And then I held my first great-grandson, Peyton,

And time stood still.

Dear Jesus, You loved little children and held them on Your knee, too. Thank You for blessing us with the infusion of grandchildren, great-grandchildren, and small friends into our lives, to keep our spirits young as we age.

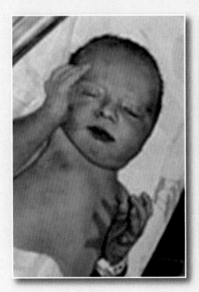 

"Jesus said, 'Let the little children come to me, and do not hinder them,
for the kingdom of heaven belongs to such as these.'"

Matthew 19:14 NIV

THAT'S MY ABBY!

Grins and giggles and golden curls,
Running and dancing with whirly twirls,
Playing games with other girls!
That's my Abby!

Swimming pools and all ball fields,
Riding anything with wheels,
Entertaining at family meals!
That's my Abby!

Praying prayers and singing loud,
Even when she's in a crowd!
She can be sunshine or a stormy cloud!
That's my Abby!

She can laugh, she can cry, she can pout with the best,
But with hugs and with kisses, she's above all the rest,
With a smile that extends from the east to the west!
That's my Abby!

Whether indoors or outdoors, she's always lots of fun,
Playing with J. T. or brother Peyton.
Wherever she is, she's a bright ray of sun!
That's my Abby!

Peacefully sleeping on Mimi's lap,
Exhausted from playing, they both need a nap!
Her Poppy, too, she also zapped!
That's my Abby!

Thank You, God, for this child so sweet!
She's a beautiful blessing and also a treat
To everyone she happens to meet!
That's my Abby!

My first great-granddaughter!
I love you, Abby!

Thank you, God, for this precious gift.

"Grandchildren are the crown of the aged, and the glory of children is their parents."

Proverbs 17:6 NRSV

A PRAYER FOR J.T.

O Dear Lord, Father of all,
We come before You on this glorious day
With thanksgiving for the countless blessings
You shower upon us daily, which we usually ignore.
Forgive our spiritual blindness.

Today, however, we cannot ignore the blessing of
The birth of not so little J. T.,
A priceless treasure presented to his parents,
Who were personally chosen by their Creator
To be his proud earthly parents.

O Lord, we pray that his home be filled with
Joy, Peace, Love, Health, Patience, and Laughter -
Lord, lots of laughter!
The Bible tells us that "Laughter does good, like a medicine,"
And we believe it!

And when his parents have not slept a wink
Because J. T. has cried all night,
And they get up cross and crabby and snappy with each other and J. T.,
May they not make mountains out of mole hills because of fatigue,

But look instead for any humor in the situation
And learn to laugh at themselves and each other.

Lord, we look at J. T. and realize that under his thin skin
You put every system he will need for the rest of his life
When You knitted him together in his mother's womb!
Wow!
We also realize that J. T. is a miraculous little sponge,
Ready to soak up everything he experiences in the home.
Scary!

If he finds love of God and each other, honesty,
Respect, kindness, happiness, forgiveness, discipline,
Responsibility, and helping others in need,
These will be a part of his character.
But if J. T.'s home is filled with anger, impatience,
Selfishness, dishonesty, disrespect, distrust, despair,
Insecurity, lack of discipline and responsibility,
J.T. will be known for these qualities.

Lord, we pray that You will guard the doors of his home,
So that all who enter – relatives or friends - will be positive influences,
Encouraging, uplifting, inspiring, helping him and his parents to be their very best!

But we know that sometimes bad people or negatives knock at the door.
Lord, when this happens, help his parents to understand that
Bad decisions are made every day by both bad people and good people
Who think there is no need to pray about little things.
Yet, while God created the vast universe,
He is also God of small things, like J.T.

May You equip his family with Your wisdom and Your understanding
Of what is right and what is wrong when making tough decisions,
For in today's world, the lines are often blurred,
Dear Lord, enable them to cope with any situation
That threatens to harm their home, themselves, or their family.

May each parent spend time individually with J. T.,
And also, as his loving parents.
May they laugh together as they help him to grow and develop.
He is going to be hilarious with his antics!
May each take time to listen to him, teach him,
Read to him, sing to him, play fun games and go fun places,
Pray with him, tell him Bible stories and take him to church.

And when J. T. grows up and starts a home of his own,
May he want to pattern it just like the one he grew up in,
Because it was there he found fun, friendship, stability, peace. trust, support,
Self-discipline, forgiveness, love, a servant's heart, and God!

Lord, help all parents to always put You first in their lives
And in their busy schedules each day.
Even as their feet hit the floor in the morning,
May they be thanking You for Your daily blessings,
Lifting their hearts in prayer,
And searching Your Word for guidance.

Wrap Your loving arms around this family, Lord. Be with all families every minute of every day, as You promised. And fill them with the joy of Your Salvation!

Amen

"Start children off on the way they should go, and even when they are old, they will not turn from it."

Proverbs 22:6 NIV

BLESSINGS CONTINUE

My husband, Clark, is a few years younger than I am. A funny thing happened when he came to my home to pick me up for our first "real" date. I had just had a birthday, and on a table I had matched my cards to the pictures of my adult grandchildren. He picked up a picture and asked, "Is this your daughter?"

"No," I replied. "That is my granddaughter, Megan." He replaced the picture.

Picking up another picture, he asked, "Is this your son?"

Taking the picture from him, I said, "No. That is my granddaughter, Nyela's husband, Brad. This one is my granddaughter, Natalie."

Looking somewhat puzzled, he commented, "I don't have any grandchildren!"

I laughed as I shoved another card in his face and said, "You don't know how old I am, do you?" The card read, "Happy 70th Birthday!"

He looked a little sheepish and said, "Well, I guess at our age it doesn't make any difference, does it?"

"I guess not." I replied, and we headed out to dinner on our first date.

Shortly after that conversation I became a great-grandmother, and he still had no grandchildren of his own. However, when we married, I gained a brother-in-law, Jim, a daughter-in-law, Maria and her husband, Lee, as well as a son-in-law, Allen and his wife, Rachelle. What blessings they are! It was only a few years later that Clark became a proud grandpa himself. Now he has two precious granddaughters, Leah and Zena, and most recently, a handsome new grandson, Lucas. They love their grandpa, and he just beams with pride! We feel so blessed to be a part of a "four-generation family!" Each member enriches our lives in his or her unique way and fills our hearts with love and joy!

However, I cannot bask in the warm glow of my family's love and ignore the countless individuals who have no one to love, or who feel totally unloved or unlovable themselves, for whatever reason. Self-contained love at another's expense is not really love, because love is meant to be shared with those less fortunate. God can become visible and bring joy to the desolate if those of us who are so very blessed will use our God-given energy and talents to alleviate the pain, suffering and loneliness of those who feel isolated from society and God. God has a wonderful plan for rescuing those who are hurting. We are that plan! May our "family" continue to expand as we remember that we are "blessed to be a blessing," as the old saying goes.

Thank You, God, for the blessings of love and family! Help us to share this joy with those who have never experienced it.

"A father to the fatherless, a defender of widows is God in his holy dwelling.

God sets the lonely in families."

Psalm 68:5, 6 NIV

HAWK ON THE STEEPLE

My thoughts were troubled as I turned left on the street that led to the back parking lot of Wesley Memorial United Methodist Church, where I was music director. We were about midway through rehearsals for our annual Christmas Dinner Theater presentation to our church and the community. Previous dinners had been quite successful, but this year rehearsals were not going well. A critical spirit was creeping through the cast, with mumbling and grumbling among our capable, dedicated singers. The music was harmonious, but relationships were not. As the group's leader, I assumed the blame, but I was clueless as to what I should do.

As I approached the parking lot, my eyes glanced to the highest point of the sanctuary roof. I saw a huge bird perched there. After parking the car, I approached a stranger, who was changing his tire in the parking lot, and asked what kind of bird that was. He had also observed it, and he told me that it was a brown hawk, which probably weighed forty pounds.

As I stood gazing at the hawk, I was distracted by a raucous sound just past the church property. In a tree were two large crows having a heated "crow" conversation. Obviously upset, they were cawing and squawking as only crows can do! Suddenly, they took flight and headed straight for the hawk on the steeple, screeching as they flew.

Together they attacked the hawk again and again, diving straight toward him, then veering off for another attack. Each attack was accompanied by the crows' entire vocabulary of caws and squawks. To my amazement, the hawk did not move a muscle. No feather was ruffled. He sat on the peak of the roof like a stone statue.

Seeing that no progress was being made, the crows retreated to their tree, where the first attack plan was plotted. The hawk remained motionless. After more loud discussion, they again attacked the hawk. (By this time the Pastor and entire church staff stood gazing at the drama). However, after their second failure to even get the hawk's attention, the crows flew past the hawk and across the street to more crows in the trees there.

After noisily plotting strategy, a third attack was launched by the two crows and several recruited crow friends, again without success. The hawk never moved, in spite of diving attacks amid shrieking caws. Admitting defeat, the attacking forces retreated across the street, and did not return. The hawk remained on his proud perch for some time, then calmly flew away.

I felt that I had just received a message from God Himself, played out with the hawk and crows, but what was it? I silently prayed for the meaning of what I had just witnessed. The answer instantly flashed through my mind: "STAND FIRM!"

I walked through the doors and back to my office with new resolve and confidence that God, not I, was in charge of our Christmas Dinner Theater. I was to "stand firm" amid the bickering, and God Himself would again bring peace and harmony to a unified cast, dedicated to the service of God.

God was faithful, and so was the wonderful cast, as they "stood firm" and witnessed to an enthusiastic church and community.

Almighty God, the visuals You use to reveal Yourself and will to us are amazing! Make us receptive to the countless ways we can "see" Your love, presence and will for our lives.

"You will not have to fight this battle. Take up your positions: Stand firm and see the deliverance the Lord will give you...."

2 Chronicles 20:17 NIV

DEATH THREAT

Back in the 1960's, my husband, Duard, was an Assistant Principal in a large high school. It was a turbulent time for our nation, but my husband loved his job and his students, even on difficult days. I was a teacher, but the flu bug had caught up with me, and I had been home sick for a few days, while my husband continued his usual routine of school and meetings.

One evening he was attending a school board meeting while I was home alone feeling miserable. The phone rang, and when I answered it, there was a pause before a very gruff voice asked to speak with my husband by his first name. When I asked if I could take a message for him, the caller growled, "Yeah! Tell him I'm gonna KILL him!" Then he slammed the phone down.

My stomach turned to water, and I thought I was going to faint! My fingers were trembling, and I had trouble dialing the police. They told me to try to get my husband home and that they would soon be there. I then contacted a friend, who went to the meeting and told him to go home. The police tried to comfort me by saying that a criminal probably would not have forewarned him if he intended to follow through with the threat. After thoroughly checking the house and premises, the police left.

My husband went to bed and promptly went to sleep. Sleep, however, would not visit me! I lay in bed letting my imagination run wild. I finally got out of bed and went to another room to read my Bible. I started reading the Psalms. Psalm 4:8 fairly jumped off the page to me and brought peace and sleep!

Thank You, Lord, for becoming visible to me each time you visit me with the right scripture at the right moment!

"I will both lay me down in peace, and sleep: for thou, Lord, only makest me dwell in safety."

Psalm 4:8 KJV

PRE-FLIGHT PANIC

The day finally arrived! We prayed, as usual, before a trip. The plane left Tennessee, bound for Atlanta. Our group included Duard, my husband, a recently widowed friend and her three daughters, plus several students from the local high school choir, which included our daughter, Melanie, and their director—me. We would be meeting other director friends and their students in Atlanta to board an overnight flight to London. We would then spend the next fifteen days on a whirlwind tour of England, Switzerland, Austria, Italy, France, and Germany. What an exciting time for my family, my students and friends! What a scary time for me! I had flown many times before this – even with my students, but never abroad and never for fifteen days!

The preceding weeks had been filled with making sure that every detail of the trip had been completed successfully, yet I still felt apprehensive and ill-equipped for the responsibilities of shepherding this flock in six foreign countries, especially since I had never traveled to Europe. Fortunately, our short flight to Atlanta was very pleasant. I was able to relax, and we arrived at our terminal without incident.

We relaxed in our terminal, knowing that we had several hours in the airport before boarding our red-eye flight to London. I knew that I was traveling with great friends and students whom I trusted, so they were free to eat dinner wherever they chose in our terminal. Their culinary tastes were varied, so they scattered in all directions. I was the only one drawn to the wonderful aromas of the oriental restaurant in front of me and my group's carry-on luggage. My dinner was delicious, and soon the rest of our group wandered back to our area to wait for our flight.

Before long, I began to feel rather uncomfortable, and at first chalked it up to my fear of the unknown and my responsibility to my students for the next two weeks. Soon, however, I realized that I was wrong—very wrong! I was sick! I lost my dinner and much more. I was so weak that I could not support my head. Panic invaded my brain! What to do? What to do? How could I board a plane in my condition? My students could not go without me! I was very weak, but I pulled my Bible from my carry-on as I frantically prayed to God for help.

I don't remember searching for a particular scripture, but I found myself reading one of my favorite chapters in the entire Bible:

Psalm 139: 7-12 NIV

"Where shall I go from your Spirit? Where can I flee from your presence?
If I go up to the heavens, you are there; if I make my bed in the depths, you are there.
If I rise on the wings of the dawn, if I settle on the far side of the sea,
Even there your hand will guide me, your right hand will hold me fast.
If I say, "Surely the darkness will hide me and the light become night around me,"
Even the darkness will not be dark to you; the night will shine like the day,
For darkness is as light to you."

As I read, my panic changed to humility, awe, reverence and thanksgiving as I realized that even while I was in such a weakened physical condition, God Himself was beside me, comforting me with His ageless truth! By revealing Himself to me through His holy word, He was healing my fearful emotions, just as He would heal my body in time.

My loving, capable traveling companions managed to get me on the plane. Physically, the flight was miserable, but mentally and emotionally I was confident and at peace, because I realized that God, not I, was in charge of our group, and He was determined to bless us all with wonderful memories to relive the rest of our lives! After a few hours of sleep in our London hotel, both my body and spirit were recharged and ready for whatever God planned for the next fifteen days—and for the rest of my life!

Thank You, Lord, for your constant care, no matter what our condition may be! I will always believe that You guided my fingers to Psalm 139 that night, because I was too sick to find it!

You are indeed AWESOME, God!

"…If I go up to the heavens, you are there; if I make my bed in the depths, you are there.

If I rise on the wings of the dawn, if I settle on the far side of the sea…"

Psalm 139: 7-12 NIV

SUB-ZERO ANGEL

Br-r-r-r-r! It was several degrees below zero, and the frigid air almost took my breath as I stepped outside to drive to a local hospital. I am a Volunteer Lay Chaplain, and it is my pleasure to visit mothers and new babies in the Birth Center each Friday morning.

It was a beautiful morning, in spite of the cold, and my spirits were high when I later finished my rounds and walked through the doors and headed for my car in the parking lot and to a warm home. I was facing a wide loading/unloading zone in front of the entrance, which narrowed to parking spaces on either side and formed a U shape. I glanced to the left lot, where my car was parked, and noticed a vehicle driving toward the hospital.

I knew I had plenty of time to safely cross the loading zone, yet as I approached the far side, the vehicle I was watching came to the end of the parking lot and turned its wheels directly toward me, instead of the wide area behind me! I was just a few feet away and remember thinking that the driver must be looking for a parking place to my right.

I thought that my time had come to leave this world and instinctively started to run backward to escape the impact. However, in my panic to retreat, I tripped and fell, with my back and head striking the concrete. I think I must have screamed, because the driver was able to stop without hitting me.

Just as I landed, the hospital doors behind me opened, and an angel (or a person sent directly from God on an angelic mission) exited the building. She was pulling a rolling tote and headed straight to me. She knelt over me and said, "Don't move! Don't move!" I obeyed and tried not to move a muscle. She immediately unzipped her tote, pulled out a heavy blanket and spread it over me in the sub-zero morning! She remained at my side until a medical team arrived on the scene. It was her blanket that lifted me onto the stretcher when a backboard could not be located immediately. I was soon whisked away to the ER. Weeks of recovery followed with the help of family and friends, and with the care of a very wise and patient Chiropractor-friend named Howard, I made a full recovery!

Someone retrieved the angel's blanket from the ER that day, but I never was able to learn her name or thank her for her kindness at just the right moment. However, these many years later I still thank God for sending her!

Thank You, God, for your presence in the time of trouble, perfectly working out
the solutions to our problems, even before we know they exist!

"...I will command my angels concerning you, and they will take you up
in their hands so that you won't hit your foot on a stone."

Matthew 4:6 CEB

FOOD FOR THOUGHT

"You are what you eat," the saying goes,
And everyone knows, "One reaps what he sows."
Yet after enjoying a bountiful feast,
I step on the scales (that annoying beast)
To find with surprise that I've gained some weight.
Surely it's not the amount that I ate!

I walk and I diet to try to be thinner,
Then sit down once more to a fat-laden dinner.
Why do I do it day after day?
Could it be that I'm trained that way?
My membership in the Clean Plate Club
Has taught me well to put away grub.

That mystery solved, I turn on the TV
And find things most disturbing to me.
Each show seems filled with violent crime,
No matter the day, no matter the time.
And that's just the newscasts I'm talking about.
There is more that's much worse, day in and day out!

How did our world get so bent out of shape,
With terrorists, murders, kidnapping and rape?
Why do we hear of this day after day?
Could it be that we're trained that way?
The diet of our children is much more than food.
It's TV, games, movies and music that's crude.

"Garbage in, garbage out" is another cliché
That reminds us to feed on the good things each day.
We must not train our children to kill
By filling their minds with violent swill.
A diet rich in joy, peace, goodness and love
Is the diet sent to us by the Father above.

Dear God, help us to remember that each day we live we must nourish our minds and souls, as well as our bodies, with wholesome thoughts and actions, if we are to inherit eternal life with You.

"But the fruit of the Spirit is love, joy, peace, patience, kindness, goodness, faithfulness, gentleness, and self-control. There is no law against things like this."

Galatians 5:22-23 CEB

GIVE THANKS

Each day begins with a prayer to God,
(Though some folks might think that's quite odd!)
But I love to read and pray, then be still
To listen as He reveals His will.

Sometimes it's so easy on a golden fall day
To sing His praises and walk in His way.
For blessings flow in endless measure,
And I know His love is my greatest treasure!

But some bleak mornings when my heart is sad,
Burdened with grief when times are bad,
It's hard to read and pray, then be still,
For in this situation I can't find His will.

But I pick up The Book and read words from Paul.
"Give thanks in all circumstances", he writes to all,
"For this is God's will for you." "For me?
My heart is broken, Lord, can't You see?

How can I give thanks when the world's all wrong?"
"Just lean on me, child, and I'll make you strong!
When you're at your weakest My power is revealed.
Your burden's too great for just one soul to wield.

So lift up your eyes, and put on a smile,
And I will walk with you each step and each mile.
Together we'll go through this valley you dread
And come out tomorrow to sunshine ahead.

Your vision today is cloudy, unclear,
But I can see joy for those I hold dear.
The good plans I have are eternal and sure
For all who accept Me with love that is pure.

So, in all things give thanks and pray without ceasing!
Rejoice evermore, and your life will be pleasing
To suffering souls that I place in your way,
As you reach out to them to brighten their day!"

Dear Father, I thank You for giving me a heart that can rejoice and a thankful spirit, regardless of the circumstances in my life, each time I remember to ask You for these marvelous gifts.

"Rejoice always. Pray continually. Give thanks in every situation
because this is God's will for you in Christ Jesus."

1 Thessalonians 5:16–18 CEB

THANKSGIVING DAY CONTRASTS

Thanksgiving is celebrated in contrasting ways,
Or not at all—just like other days.
Some look forward to family fun,
While others are sad, for they have no one.

Morning dawns on Thanksgiving Day
As a child of God passes away.
Yet a new-born baby finds its first cry
As Mother and Daddy rejoice nearby.

A loving family at breakfast prays
For peace throughout the world always,
While others plot to maim and slay
All who do not think as they.

Ice and snow and rain and sleet
Send some to the fireplace to warm their feet.
But faraway farmers plow and sow,
And vacationers bask in the sun's warm glow.

A young child grows tall with love and instruction
In treating all others with love and affection.
But next door are neglect, abuse and pain,
As a child's soul is tortured again and again.

What can we say? What can we do?
We live in a world of contrasts. It's true!
Some contrasts are good, but others are not,
It's up to us to discover "What's what!"

We cannot be complacent and shut our eyes tight
And pretend in the end it will turn out all right!
Some things are right, but some things are wrong.
We cannot ignore wrong and just go along!

We must be involved! We must be aware!
We must let those hurting know that we care.
So, let us stand firm and strengthen our nerve
And let the world know that we're here to serve.

As our families meet this Thanksgiving Day
And join hands before we pray,
Let us study the contrasts on the table before us:
The colors the textures, aromas and flavors

Combined to delight us and bring us pleasure.
Fun and fellowship without measure!
This problem of contrasts can be solved,
But only if all become involved!

By bringing our differences to the table of love
And presenting them to our Father above,
We can witness the beauty of His vast creation,
And our world can be healed, nation by nation!

*Dear Father, it is very hard to understand the stark contrasts we face in this world daily. Lead us
in ministry to Your less fortunate children whom You love just as much as You love us.*

:… Love your neighbor as yourself."

Matthew 22:39 NIV

CHANGE

Change is inevitable, don't you think?
From childhood to old age with hardly a blink!
Where has the time gone? I don't know.
With each passing day, it accelerates so!

Our landscapes have changed from farmland so green
To towering cities where multitudes team,
With lives so filled with hustle and bustle
That even best friends cause our feathers to ruffle.

We run here and there with scarcely a thought.
Our houses are packed with things we have bought.
Our bodies have changed, and our hair may be white.
It seemed to have happened just overnight!

Technology baffles and leaves us behind,
And looking around, I can't say that I mind.
I'll use what I can to serve God the best,
And let others more knowledgeable deal with the rest!

We now must face illness, fatigue – even loss.
Our brains and our bank accounts shoulder the cost.
Our daily routines are harder to follow –
The bitterest pill of all we must swallow!

Yet we really have no need to mope or to cry,
Or sulk in our homes, and I'll tell you why!
God is our Constant when change is so great,
And He is in control – not fate!

With compassion and love His strength He will give
As He calls us to service each day that we live!
He puts in our path the young and the old.
We make their lives better through our servant role.

Our faith increases, and hope returns
As our love pours out to those who yearn
For a smile, a friend, food or fun.
Reach out to others, and the battle is won!

So, let's welcome change! Make it our friend!
And we can be young till our journey's end.
To go somewhere, we must leave somewhere.
So just trust in God. He will lead us there.

Lord, help us to accept the changes we face in our lives, that we may more closely follow Your leading.

"Not that I speak in regard to me, for I have learned in whatever state I am, to be content."

Philippians 4:11 NKJV

Printed in the United States
By Bookmasters